1/16/84

To Lisa
With lots, lots of
love
Nana

Toronto Canada

HIS HOLINESS
POPE JOHN PAUL II
IN CELEBRATION OF HIS VISIT

Royce PUBLICATIONS

HIS HOLINESS POPE JOHN PAUL II
In celebration of his visit

The following is a pictorial record of a previous visit made
to this continent by Pope John Paul II. The response by
Canadians to his presence in our country can be reflected
in the multitude of people who responded to his warm
personality and stirring messages delivered to our
American neighbours, as depicted herewith.

Arrival – Boston

"...America has opened her heart to me. And on my part, I come to you, America, with sentiments of friendship, reverence and esteem. I come as one who already knows you, and loves you, as one who wishes you to fulfill completely your noble destiny of courage to the world."

"...Permit me to express my sentiments in the lyrics of your own song: 'America, America, God shed His Grace on thee. And crown thy good with brotherhood, from sea to shining sea.'

And may the peace of the Lord be with you always, America."

3

...To all of you I extend – in the name of Christ – the call, the invitation, the plea: 'Come and follow me.' This is why I have come to America, and why I have come to Boston tonight: to call you to Christ – to call all of you and each of you to live in his love, today and forever. Amen!"

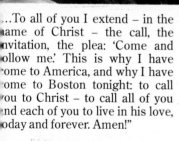

"...I desire to express my gratitude to the General Assembly of the United Nations, which I am permitted today to participate in and to address.

My thanks go in the first place to the Secretary General of the United Nations Organization, Dr. Kurt Waldheim. Last autumn, soon after my election to the chair of St. Peter, he invited me to make this visit, and he renewed his invitation in the course of our meeting in Rome last May.

From the first moment, I felt greatly honored and deeply obliged. And today, before this distinguished assembly, I also thank you, Mr. President, who has so kindly welcomed me and invited me to speak."

"...The formal reason for my intervention today is, without any question, the special bond of cooperation that links the Apostolic See with the United Nations Organization, as is shown by the presence of the Holy See permanent observer to this organization.

Besides attaching great importance to its collaboration with the United Nations Organization, the Apostolic See has always since the foundation of your organization expressed its esteem and its agreement with the historic significance of this supreme forum for the international life of humanity today.

It also never ceases to support your organization's functions and initiatives which are aimed at peaceful coexistence and collaboration between nations.

● ● ●

"Now, availing myself of the solemn occasion of my meeting with the representatives of the nations of the earth, I wish above all to send my greetings to all the men and women living on this planet, to every man and every woman without any exception whatever. Every human being living on earth is a member of a civil society, of a nation, many of them represented here.

● ● ●

"The progress of humanity must be measured not only by the progress of science and technology, which shows man's uniqueness with regard to nature, but also and chiefly by the primacy given to the spiritual values and the progress of moral life.

● ● ●

"Fourteen years ago, my great predecessor, Pope Paul VI, spoke from this podium. He spoke memorable words which I desire to repeat today:

'No more war. War never again. Never one against the other, or even one above the other, but always in every occasion, with each other.'

Paul VI was a tireless servant of the cause of peace. I wish to follow him with all my strength, and continue his service. The Catholic Church in every place on earth proclaims a message of peace, prays for peace, educates for peace.

This purpose is also shared by the representatives and followers of other churches and communities and of other religions of the world. And they have pledged themselves to it.

● ● ●

"I consider that the famous opening words of the Charter of the United Nations – in which the peoples of the United Nations determined to save succeeding generations from the scourge of war solemnly reaffirmed faith in fundamental human rights, in the dignity and worth of the human person, in the equal rights of men and women and of nations large and small – are meant to stress this dimension. An analysis of the history of mankind, especially at its present stage, shows how important is the duty of revealing more fully the range of the goods that are linked with the spiritual dimension of human existence. It shows how important this task is for building peace and how serious is any threat to human rights. Any violation of them even in a peace situation is a form of warfare against humanity.

● ● ●

"I would now like to draw attention to a second systematic threat to man in his inalienable rights in the modern world, a threat which constitutes no less a danger than the first to the cause of peace. I refer to the various forms of injustice in the field of the spirit.

Man can indeed be wounded in his inner relationship with truth in his conscience, in his most personal belief, in his view of the world, in his religious faith, and in the sphere of what are known as civil liberties. Decisive for these, these last, is equality of rights without discrimination on grounds of origin, race, sex, nationality, religion, political convictions and the like.

For centuries, the thrust of civilization has been in one direction – that of giving the life of individual political societies a form in which there can be fully safeguarded the objective rights of the spirit of human conscience and of human creativity, including man's relationship with God.

● ● ●

"It is a question of the highest importance that in internal social life as well as in international life, all human beings in every nation and country should be able to enjoy effectively their full rights under any political regime or system. Only the safeguarding of this real completeness of rights for every human being, without discrimination, can insure peace at its very roots.

● ● ●

"I hope that each person will live and grow strong with the moral force of the community that forms its members as citizens. I hope that the state authorities, while respecting the just rights of each citizen, will enjoy the confidence of all for the common good.

I hope that all the nations, even the smallest, even those that do not yet enjoy full sovereignty, and those that have been forcibly robbed of it, will meet in full equality with the others in the United Nations Organization."

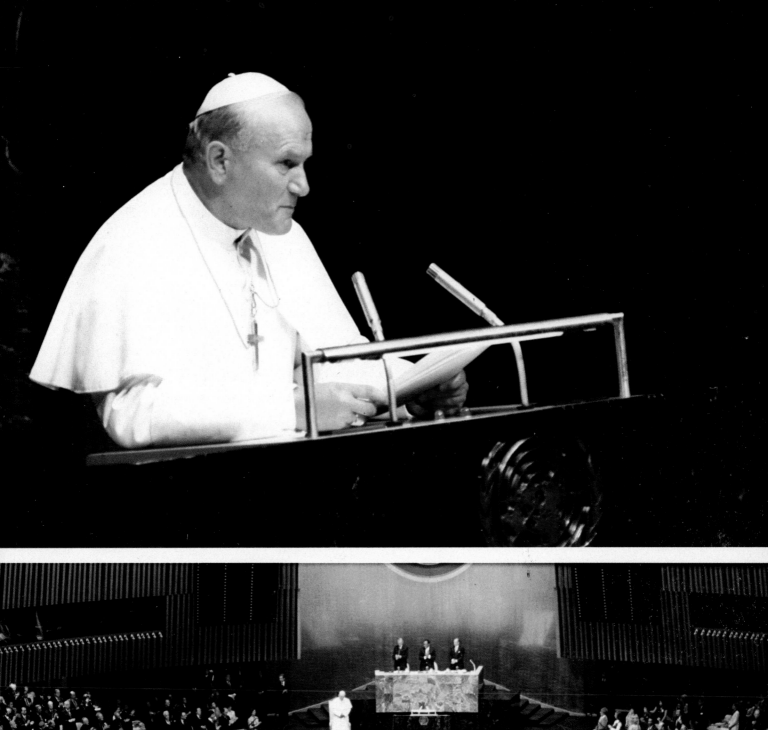

"...I hope that the United Nations will ever remain the supreme forum of peace and justice, the authentic seat of freedom of peoples and individuals in their longing for a better future."

Harlem and Bronx...

"...In this great City of New York, there live a great many immigrants of a variety of colors, races and nationalities, among which is a large community of Spanish-speaking people to whom I now direct myself.

I came here because I know the difficult conditions of your existence, because I know the sorrow that takes place in your lives. For this reason, you deserve particular attention on the part of the Pope."

Yankee Stadium . . .

"...Christ demands openness to our brothers and sisters in need – openness from the rich, the affluent, the economically advanced; openness to the poor, the underdeveloped and the disadvantaged. Christ demands an openness that is more than benign attention, more than token actions or half-hearted efforts that leave the poor as destitute as before or even more so."

"...And so, in the name of the solidarity that binds us all together in a common humanity, I again proclaim the dignity of every human person: the rich man and Lazarus are both human beings, both of them equally created in the image and likeness of God, both of them equally redeemed by Christ, at a great price, the price of 'the precious blood of Christ'."

"...Brothers and sisters in Christ, with deep conviction and affection I repeat to you the words that I addressed to the world when I took up my apostolic ministry in the service of all men and women: 'Do not be afraid. Open wide the doors for Christ. To his saving power open the boundaries of states, economic and political systems, the vast fields of culture, civilization and development. Do not be afraid. Christ knows what is in man; He alone knows it.'"

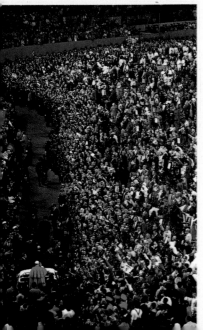

Lineups

Visitors   Yankees   Umpires

10/2/79

POPE JOHN PAUL

Madison Square Garden . . .
"...Dear young people, you and I and all of us together make up the church. And we are convinced that only in Christ do we find real love and the fullness of life. And so I invite you today to look to Christ.

When you wonder about the mystery of yourself, look to Christ, who gives you the meaning of life. When you wonder what it means to be a mature person, look to Christ, who is the fullness of humanity. And when you wonder about your role in the future of the world and of the United States, look to Christ."

Even the heavy rain that soaked the crowd-thronged sidewalks could not dampen the enthusiastic, traditional ticker-tape welcome to New York on the Pope's historic visit.

When the Pope arrived at St. Patrick's Cathedral at 8.25 am, for a service that had been specially set aside for those whose vocation lies in the service of the church, he was met by eager crowds, many of whom had waited since the early hours of the misty morning.

In his brief sermon the Pope praised the practice of morning prayer as "a joyful communal celebration of God's love in Christ," to the 3,000 priests, brothers and nuns gathered in St. Patrick's Cathedral.

Shea Stadium . . .

"...From Rome I bring you a message of faith and love: 'May the peace of Christ reign in your hearts!' Make peace the desire of your heart, for if you love peace you will love all humanity, without distinction of race, color or creed."

● ● ●

"Keep Jesus Christ in your hearts, and you will recognize His face in every human being. You will want to help Him out in all His needs: the needs of your brothers and sisters."

"...I pray for you, for your families and friends, above all for your children, for the sick and suffering, and to all of you I give my blessing. May God be with you always."

"...Philadelphia is the city of the Declaration of Independence, that remarkable document, containing a solemn attestation of the equality of all human beings, endowed by their Creator with certain inalienable rights: life, liberty and the pursuit of happiness, expressing a 'firm reliance on the protection of Divine Providence'."

47

es Moines . . .
. May the simplicity of your life-
yle and the closeness of your
mmunity be the fertile ground
r a growing commitment to
sus Christ"... was the Pope's
essage from St. Patrick's
urch, near Cumming, in the
lling farmland of Iowa – his first
op before proceeding to the
pal Mass at Living History
rms, where a gathered crowd
mbered some 350,000 on a
0-acre pasture.

Blue skies and enthuiastic crowds greeted the Pope during his brief visit to Iowa, a stop that was not in the Pope's original itinerary, but was included only five weeks before the tour began, and was the result of a hand-written invitation from a Truro farmer.

Chicago...

"...Brothers in Christ: as we proclaim the truth in love, it is not possible for us to avoid all criticism; nor is it possible to please everyone. But it is possible to work for the real benefit of everyone. And so we are humbly convinced that God is with us in our ministry of truth, and that he did not give us a spirit of timidity but a spirit of power and love and self-control."

55

"...The Holy Spirit is active in enlightening the minds of the faithful with his truth, and in inflaming their hearts with his love. But these insights of faith and this sensus fidelium are not independent of the magisterium of the church, which is an instrument of the same Holy Spirit and is assisted by him.

It is only when the faithful have been nourished by the word of God, faithfully transmitted in its purity and integrity, that their own charisms are fully operative and fruitful."

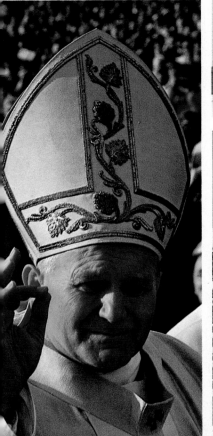

Washington . . .

". . . We cannot live without love. If we do not encounter love, if we do not experience it and make it our own, and if we do not participate intimately in it, our life is meaningless. Without love we remain incomprehensible to ourselves."

"Thus every one of you needs a vibrant relationship of love to the Lord, a profound loving union with Christ, your spouse, a love like that expressed in the psalm."

"...Human life is not just an idea or an abstraction; human life is the concrete reality of a being that lives, that acts, that grows and develops; human life is the concrete reality of a being that is capable of love, and of service to humanity."

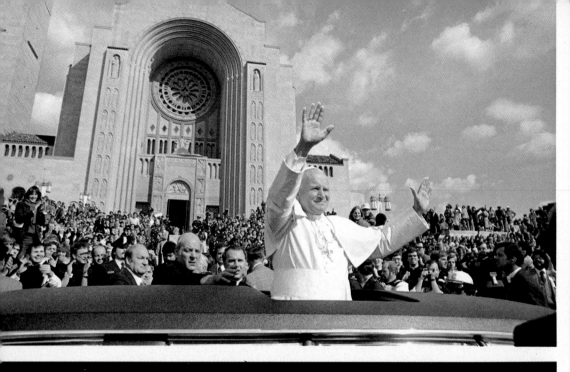

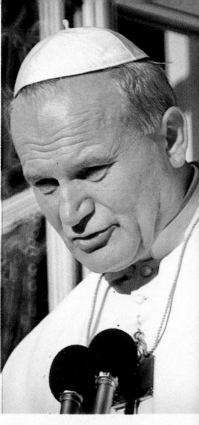

"…Mr. President, I am honored to have had, at your kind invitation, the opportunity for a meeting with you. For, by your office as President of the United States of America, you represent, before the world, the whole American nation. And you hold the immense responsibility of leading this nation in the path of justice and peace."

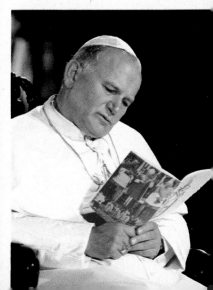

.And now I must leave the United States and return to Rome. But all of you will constantly be remembered in my prayers, which I look upon as the best expression of my loyalty and friendship.

Today, therefore, my final prayer is this: that God will bless America, so that she may increasingly become, and truly be, and long remain, 'one nation, under God, indivisible, with liberty and justice for all'."

God bless America!
God bless America!

First published by Colour Library Books Ltd.
© 1984 Illustrations: Colour Library Books Ltd. and J. W. Martin Canty
(to whom the publishers are indebted for the use of some of the pictures).
First published in Canada by Royce Publications.
Colour separation by FERCROM, Barcelona, Spain.
Display and text filmsetting by Focus Photoset, London, England.
Printed and bound by JISA-RIEUSSET, Barcelona, Spain.
ISBN 0 86283 179 2
COLOUR LIBRARY BOOKS